Sid's Nits

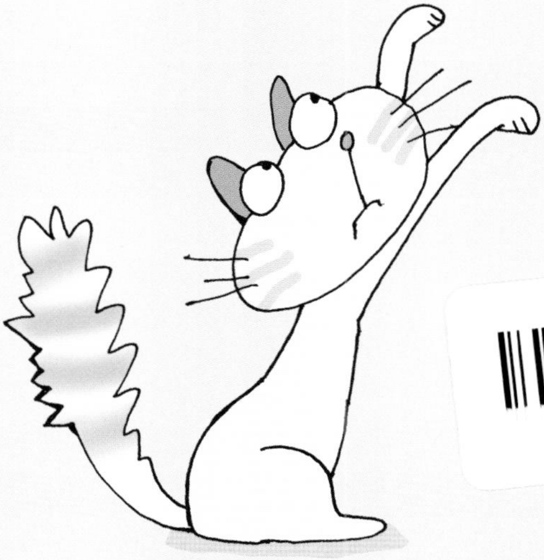

Written by Nicola Sandford
Illustrated by Jess Mikhail

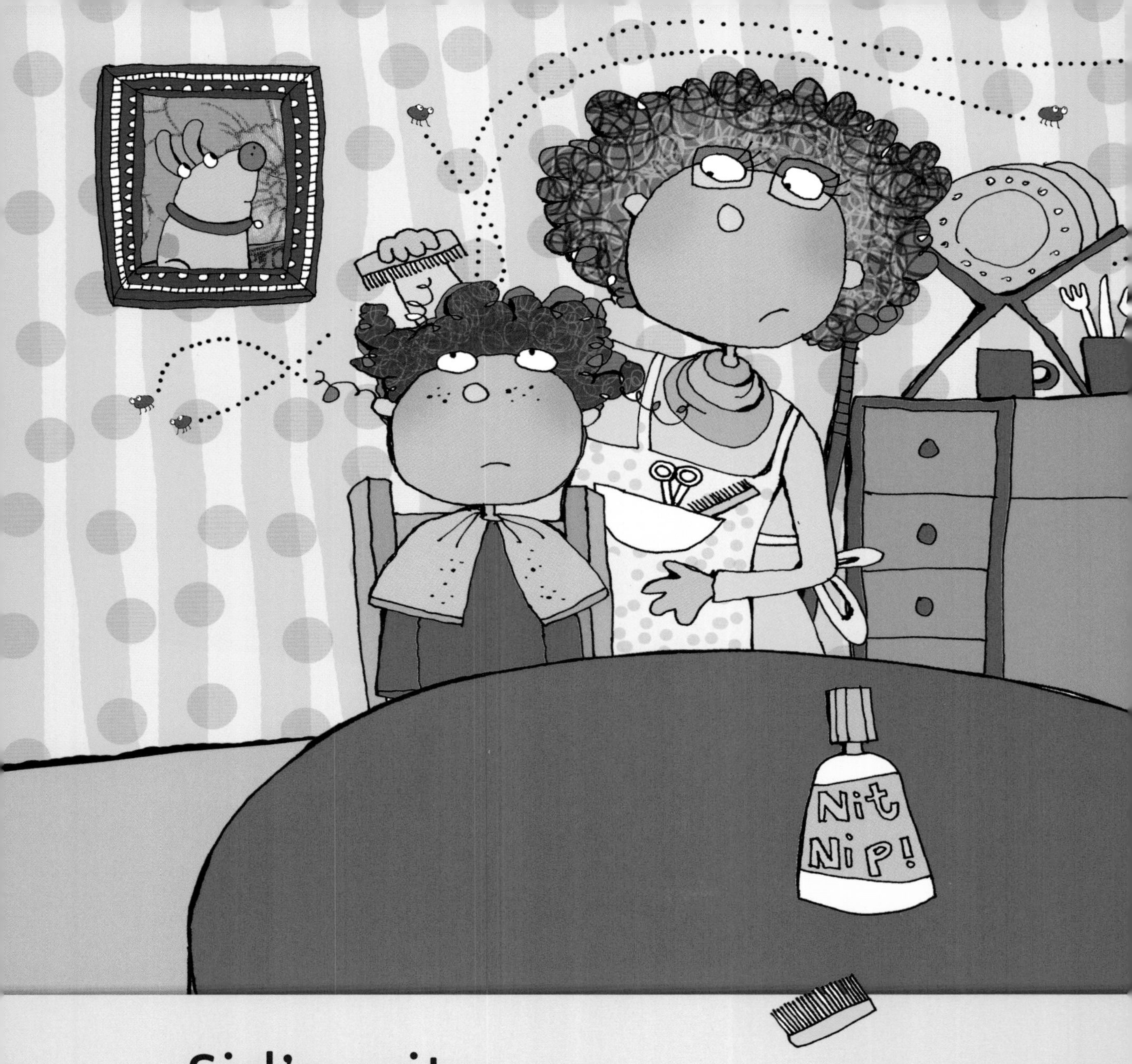

Sid's nits

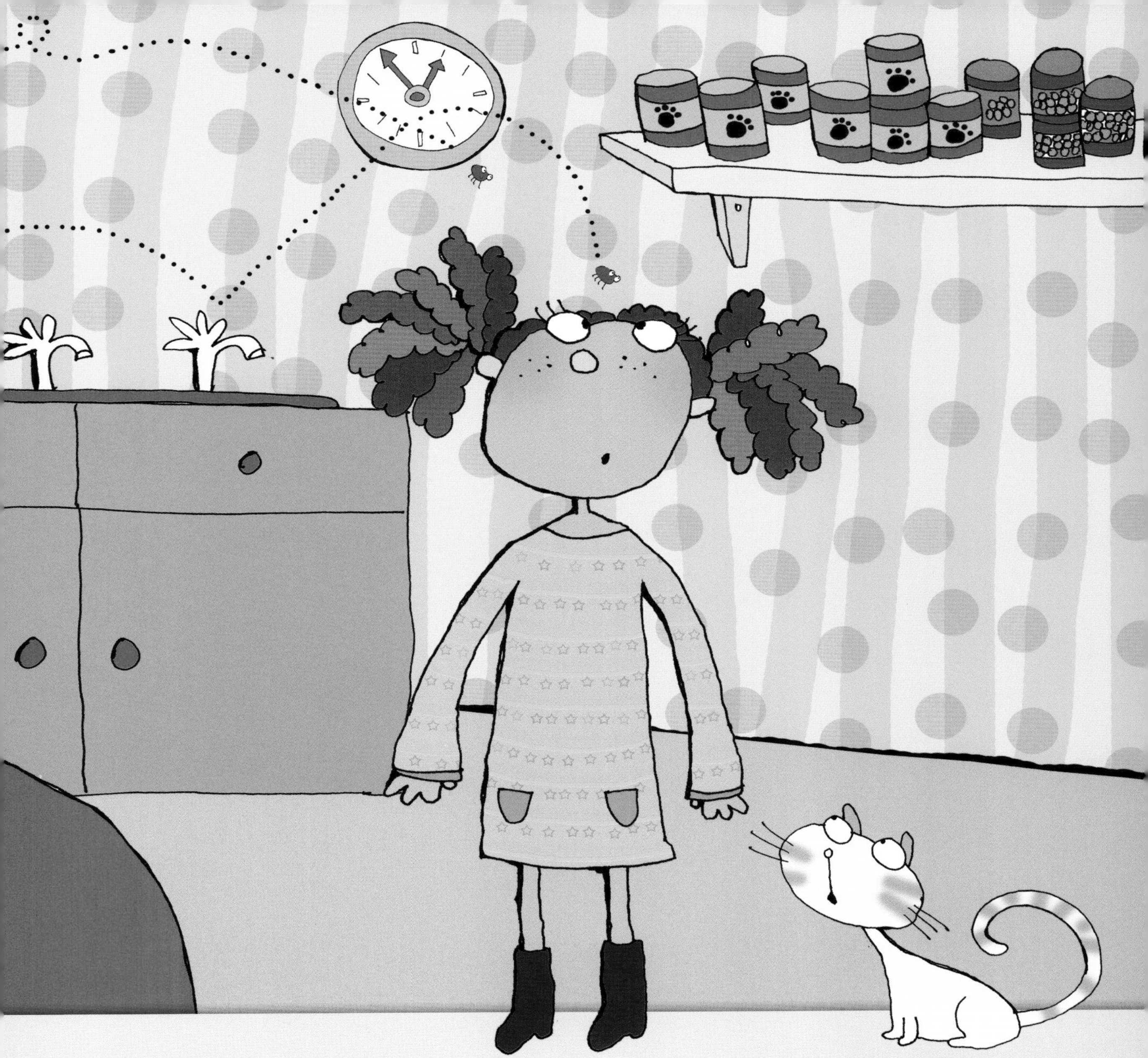

Sam's nits

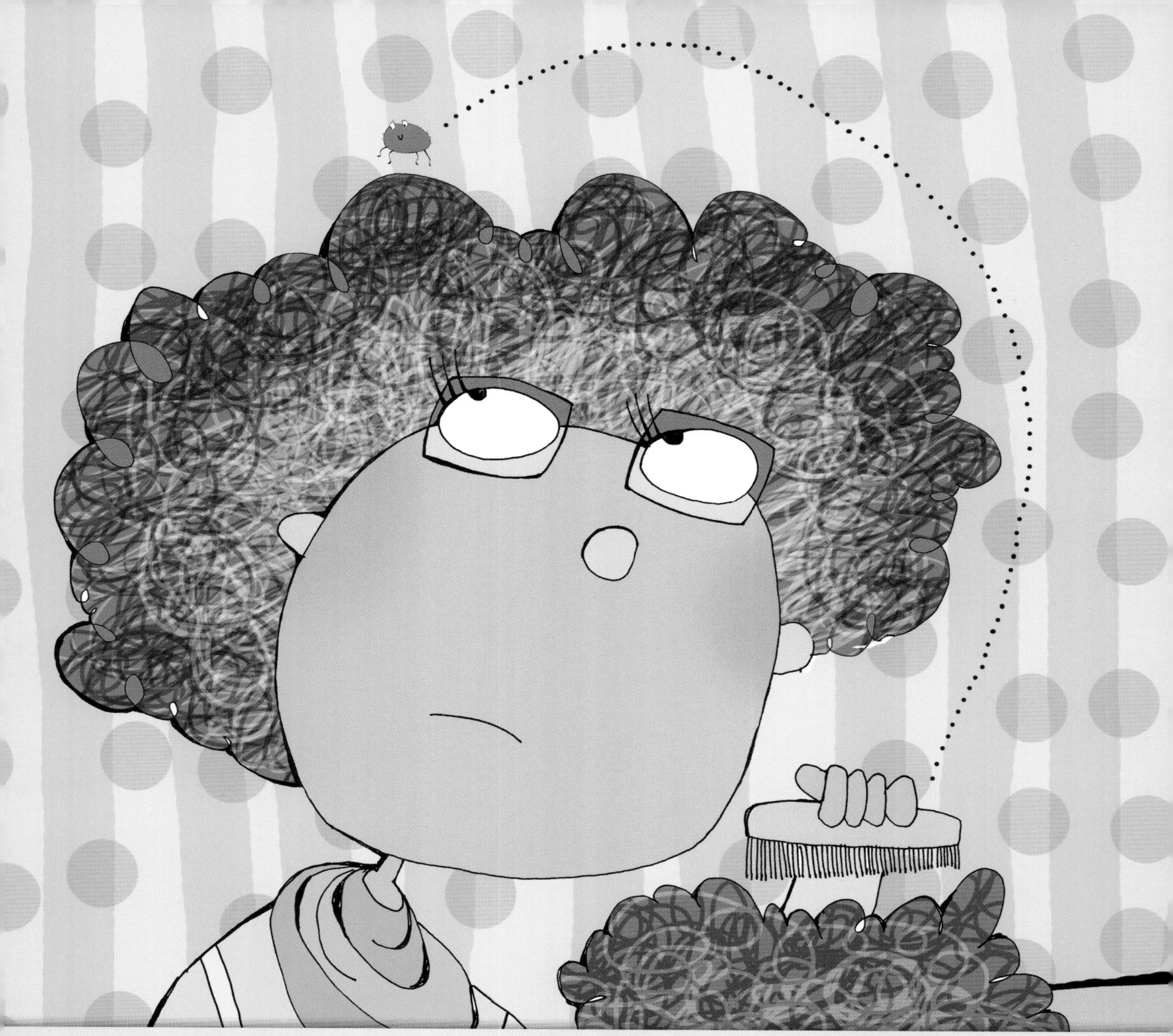

Nan's nit

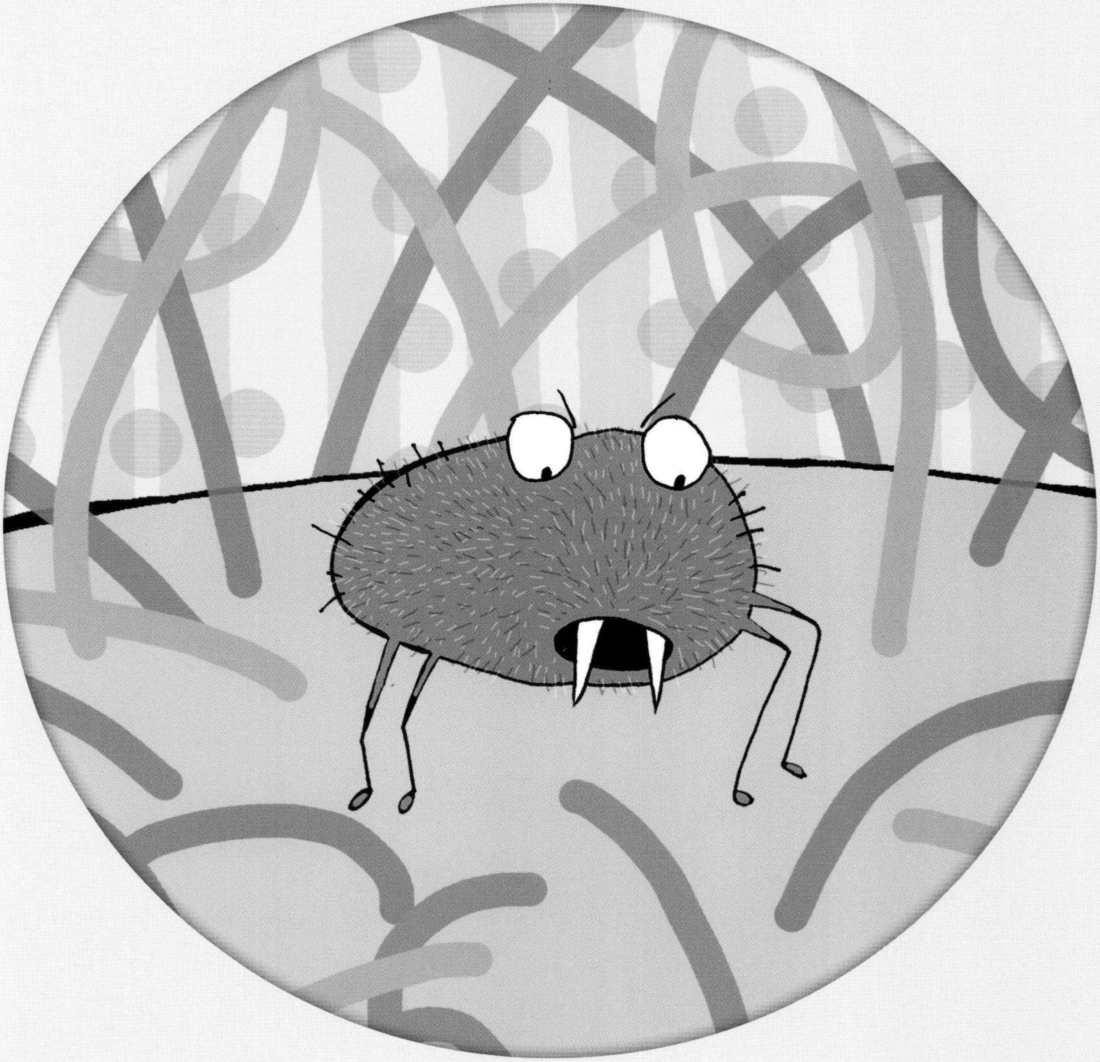

It nips Nan.

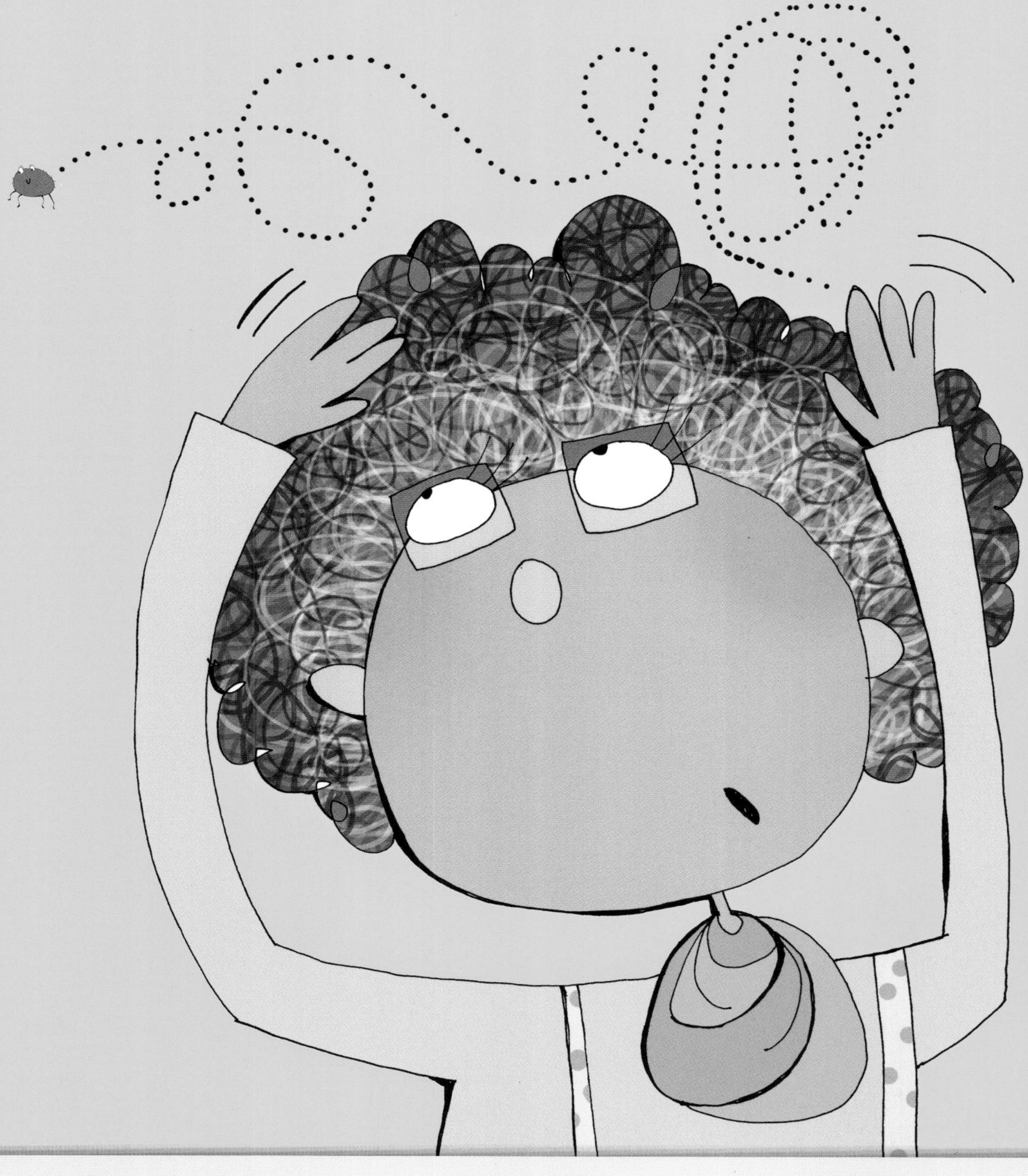

It dips.

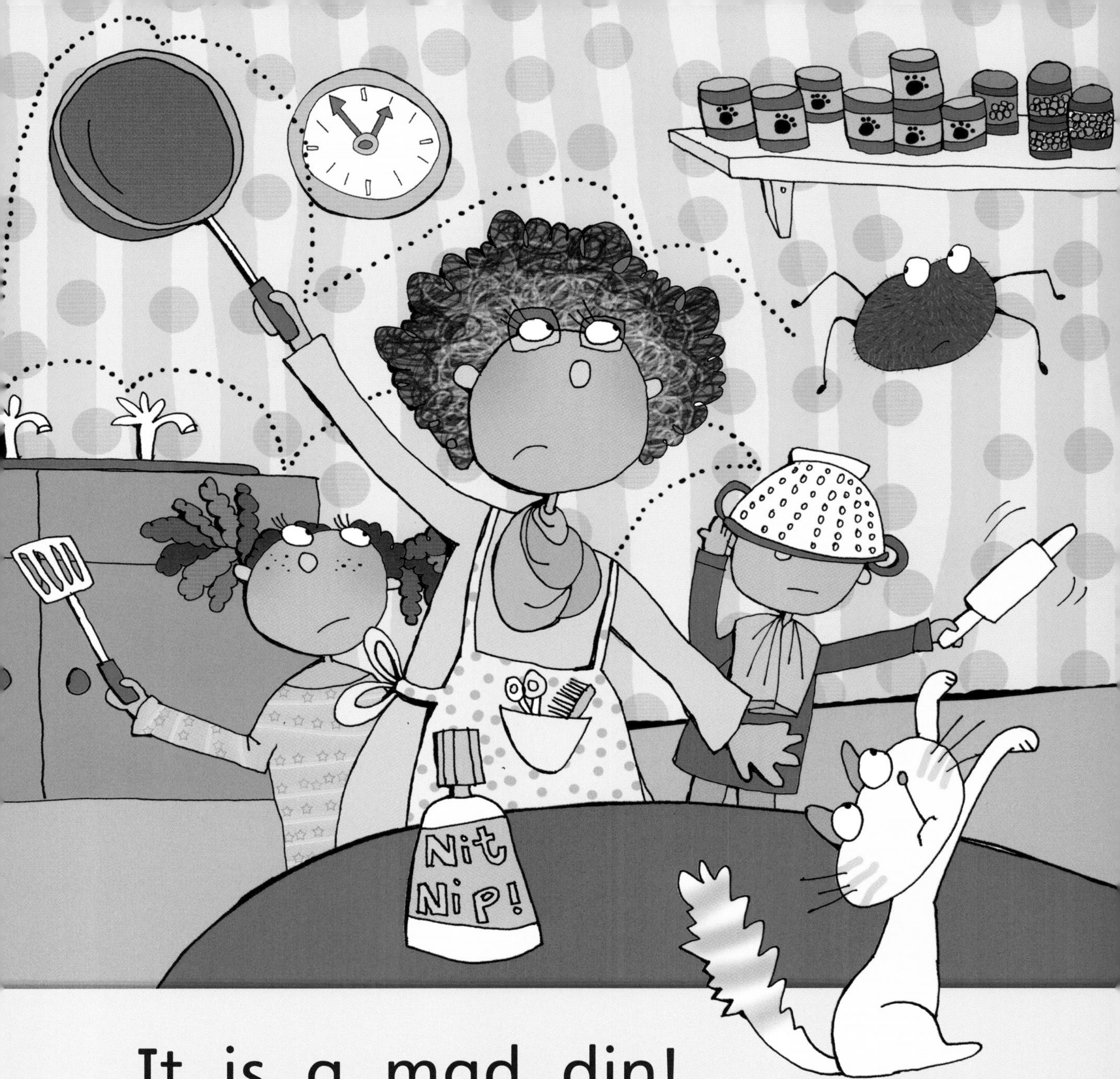

It is a mad din!

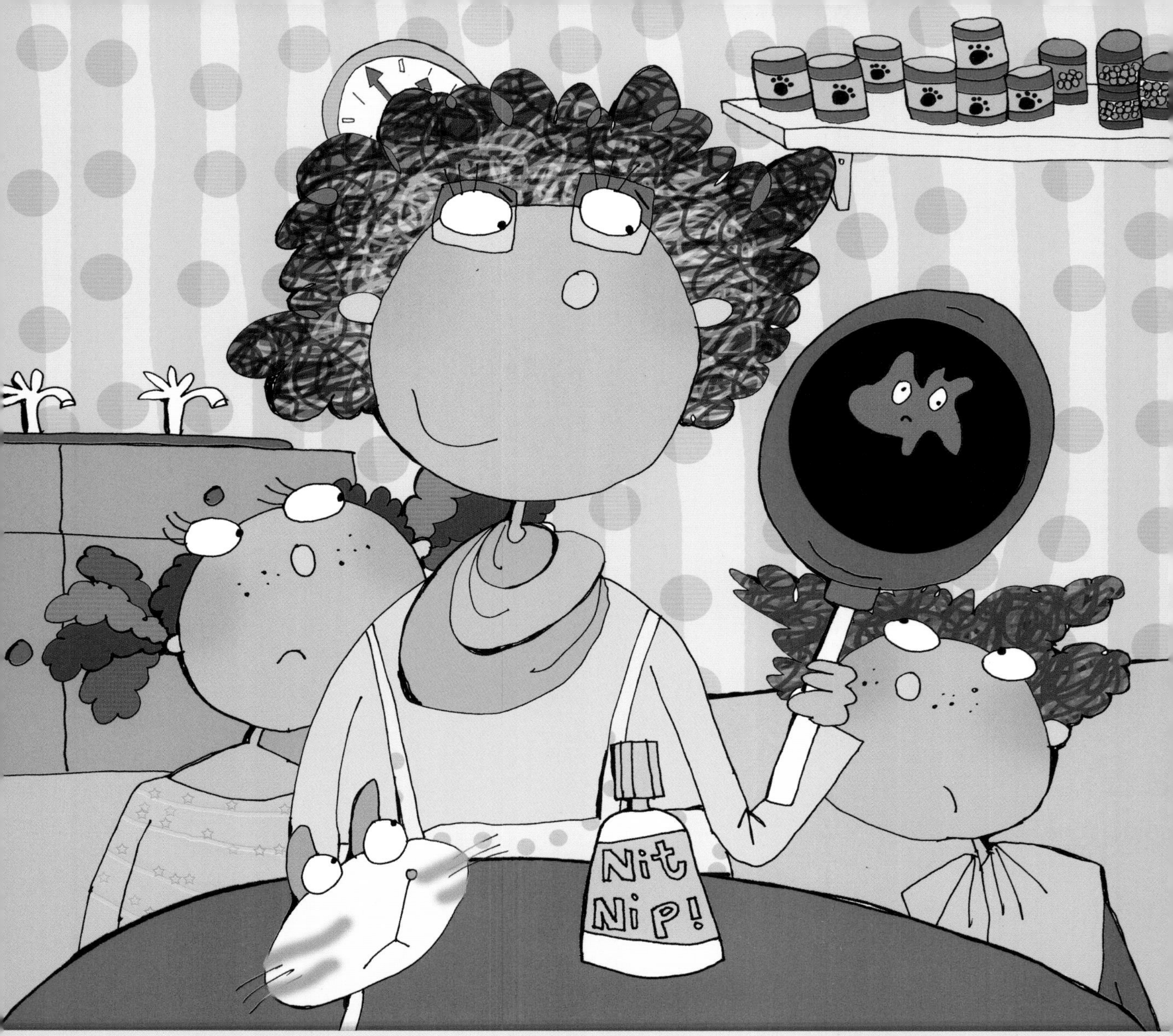

Nan's pan